Original title:
Broken Promises

Copyright © 2024 Swan Charm
All rights reserved.

Author: Olivia Orav
ISBN HARDBACK: 978-9916-79-179-0
ISBN PAPERBACK: 978-9916-79-180-6
ISBN EBOOK: 978-9916-79-181-3

Shadows of a Forgotten Pledge

In whispers lost, a vow once bright,
Fading echoes of sacred light.
When the heart strays from its course,
Hope lies buried beneath remorse.

Yet through the dark, a spark ignites,
Guiding souls to ancient heights.
In shadows deep, the promise lingers,
Held by unseen, guiding fingers.

Tattered Scriptures

Pages worn, wisdom frayed,
In the quiet, faith displayed.
Lines that bend under heavy loads,
Carry dreams and sacred codes.

Each tear speaks of battles fought,
Lessons learned and burdens caught.
In every crease, a story lives,
To the weary, solace gives.

Lingering Doubt

In the silence, whispers call,
Doubt may rise, yet faith stand tall.
Questions hang in the dusky air,
Seeking truth, a cautious prayer.

With trembling hands, we reach for grace,
Finding light in the darkest place.
In uncertainty, we still believe,
In fragile hearts, hope will cleave.

The Unspoken Lament of Faith

Beneath the surface, sorrows flow,
In hearts unseen, a silent woe.
Though lips are sealed in solemn thrall,
The spirit cries, answering the call.

Through trials faced and shadows cast,
Enduring storms that chill the vast.
In unvoiced tears, the faith remains,
A glimpse of grace in hidden strains.

Shards of an Oath Crumbled

Promises once strong now lie scattered,
Dreams forgotten, hopes once flattered.
Yet in each shard, a flicker glows,
Reminding us of what we chose.

Mending hearts with tender care,
Rebuilding trust in quiet prayer.
Though fractured paths we walk alone,
The oath may break, but love is sown.

Visions Muted by the Night

In shadows deep, our faith shall grow,
With whispered prayers, the heart will glow.
Each moment spent lost in the dark,
Shall guide the soul to find its spark.

The nightingale sings to the stars,
A beacon of hope, despite the scars.
In silence, we seek the light above,
Finding solace in the essence of love.

Guided by dreams of ethereal grace,
In twilight's embrace, we find our place.
As dawn breaks softly, the truth is clear,
In the muted night, the divine draws near.

Through the veil of doubt, our spirits rise,
With courage born from whispered sighs.
In every struggle, in every plight,
The visions unfold, muted by night.

The Cost of Disillusionment's Grace

In shadows cast by broken trust,
We seek the path of love, we must.
Disillusionment whispers softly here,
Yet grace abides, and wipes the tear.

The weight of truth exceeds our pride,
In humility, we must abide.
What price we pay for faith reborn,
In the depths of night, new hopes are sworn.

Each step we take, a lesson learned,
In ashes of dreams, our hearts have burned.
Yet spirit soars beyond despair,
In every wound, the light we bear.

Resilience blooms in barren ground,
In silence, the sacred is found.
While disillusion may dim our view,
In grace, anew, our hopes break through.

In the Ruins of Sacred Trust

Among the stones where faith once stood,
We walk with hearts both brave and good.
In ruins left by time's cruel hand,
We seek the promise of a new land.

With every breath, the memories ache,
Yet from the ashes, we shall awake.
For even in loss, a seed is sown,
In the sacred ground, our souls have grown.

Shattered dreams, like glass, may shine,
Reflecting paths where the divine entwines.
In broken places, new hope takes root,
From sorrow's soil, our spirits shoot.

Trust reborn in the midst of strife,
A testament to the strength of life.
In the ruins, we find our way,
As love leads forth, despite the gray.

Celestial Dreams, Earthly Failures

In dreams celestial, we chase the dawn,
Yet earthly failures linger on.
The stars may guide, but doubt may creep,
Through silent nights that steal our sleep.

We strive for heights where eagles soar,
Yet grounded, we face the world's uproar.
With open hearts, we seek the truth,
In every loss, the spark of youth.

Failures teach us lessons deep,
In humble moments, our spirits leap.
For in the shadows of our fears,
We find the strength that perseveres.

Celestial visions whisper sweet,
In every trial, there lies defeat.
Yet still we push toward heaven's call,
Embracing both our rise and fall.

Stained Glass and Shattered Trust

In the chapel's light, colors blend,
Promises made, but hearts descend.
Shadows whisper, faith is weak,
Truth in pieces, silence speaks.

Beneath the arch of ancient stone,
Fragile souls left all alone.
Hopes reflected in vibrant hue,
Yet the cracks reveal what's true.

With every prayer, a secret held,
In stained glass, our spirits meld.
The beauty masked by broken seals,
Faithful hearts that time reveals.

Hands once clasped in sacred bond,
Now the echoes of hearts abscond.
In holy halls, the sacred trust,
Has turned to dust, returned to dust.

when Belief Weeps for a Sinner

In the stillness of the night,
A cry for mercy, pure and bright.
Belief a river, flowing raw,
Weeping softly for the flaw.

Fallen angels claim their due,
In shadows, darkness breaks anew.
Yet a prayer lifts from the ground,
In broken vows, hope is found.

Each teardrop lands on sacred soil,
A testament of love's toil.
When sin is heavy, burdens steep,
Belief will guard, the heart will keep.

The sinner's heart, a humble plea,
In faith's embrace, we long to be.
For in repentance, grace we seek,
A gentle balm for hearts that weep.

Serpents Among the Saints

In robes of white, the actors sway,
While serpents linger, led astray.
Whispers coil in sacred space,
Deceit masked by a holy face.

In the choir, the voices rise,
Yet in the shadows, sin belies.
A serpent's charm, sweet words deceive,
In webs, the faithful can misbelieve.

Veils of piety, tattered thin,
To find the truth, we must begin.
Among the saints, the trials dwell,
In hearts entwined, we break the spell.

Faith's foundation, built on trust,
Yet serpents linger, twist to dust.
In the gathering, shadows loom,
A sacred space, a hidden tomb.

Hymns of Despair at Dusk

As daylight fades, the shadows grow,
Softly sung, our hearts laid low.
A hymn of sorrow fills the air,
In twilight's grasp, we find our despair.

With every note, the silence breaks,
In shadows deep, the spirit aches.
A melody of lost belief,
In dusk we sing our quiet grief.

The candle flickers, dimming light,
In hymns we share our darkest night.
Grace and doubt entwined in strife,
Seeking solace, seeking life.

Yet in the dusk, a hope may gleam,
Through hymns of pain, we dare to dream.
For though despair may cloud the sky,
In faith's embrace, we learn to fly.

Mosaic of Shattered Hopes

In fragments lie the dreams once bright,
Each piece a story lost in night.
A tapestry of wishes worn,
In silence, echoes of the torn.

Faded visions dance away,
Underneath the weight of gray.
Yet within these cracks, a spark,
A whisper shines against the dark.

Shattered glass reflects the light,
As broken hearts seek to ignite.
With every shard a lesson learned,
In sorrow's fire, our spirits burned.

A canvas stained with tears untold,
Yet beauty rests in the bold.
From rubble, new flowers bloom,
In the heart's garden, dispel the gloom.

For every hope that comes undone,
A phoenix rises with the sun.
In this mosaic, life's embrace,
Love endures, despite the place.

The Vaulted Ceiling of Broken Belief

Underneath the arches high,
Lies a prayer hushed, a soft sigh.
Where faith once soared beyond the sky,
Now shadows drift and echoes cry.

Walls adorned with whispers faint,
Stories carved by the saint's paint.
A sanctuary of dreams confined,
In the silence, a truth outlined.

Lost in the stillness, hearts ache,
For every promise made to break.
Yet in doubt's grip, a light stays near,
A glimmer of hope, dispelling fear.

Countless souls search for a sign,
In the ruins, a thread divine.
Each crack reveals a hidden grace,
Redemption waits in the desolate space.

Beneath the vaulted ceiling's guise,
Faith flickers still, it never dies.
Amidst the broken, a prayer rises,
In brokenness, true love surprises.

Radiance Dimmed by Disillusionment

Once the stars were bright above,
Filling hearts with endless love.
Yet shadows creep where light once played,
In dreams of trust, the faith has frayed.

The altar stands, a ghostly frame,
Where candles flicker but wane the flame.
Each prayer whispers to the void,
As once-held visions feel destroyed.

Tread softly on this hollow ground,
Where laughter lost can barely sound.
In disillusionment's cold embrace,
We seek the warmth of a familiar face.

Yet even in despair's tight hold,
A flicker of grace still shines bold.
For in the dark's unyielding night,
Hope's ember glows, a feeble light.

Though radiance may seem to fade,
In life's mosaic, love's not swayed.
Through every trial and shadow cast,
A spirit's strength will ever last.

Faith's Last Candle

In the stillness of the night,
Flickers faint a candlelight.
As shadows dance upon the wall,
It holds the weight of every fall.

A single flame against the dark,
Its fragile glow a steadfast mark.
In moments fraught with doubt and fear,
The heart still beats, the soul is near.

Around it gather whispered prayers,
For strength to face what life declares.
Through trials faced and choices made,
In holy light, our doubts are laid.

Yet time may wear the wick to naught,
And love may seem a battle fought.
But clinging tight to what we know,
In love, we find the strength to grow.

So let the candle guide us right,
Through storms that rage and darkest night.
In faith's embrace, we find our way,
Unyielding hope, come what may.

A Pilgrimage through Broken Stones

Through valleys worn by time's cruel hand,
We walk these paths, with faith not grand.
Each step a prayer, each breath a plea,
In search of solace, we seek to be free.

The stones we tread hold stories old,
Of souls who wandered, brave and bold.
Their whispers guide us, soft and clear,
As we embrace the holy fear.

In shadows cast by mountains high,
We lift our eyes to the unyielding sky.
A beacon glimmers, hope ignites,
In every heart, a spark of light.

With every falter, every fall,
We find our strength within the call.
To rise again upon this road,
Forging onward, the sacred load.

So let the broken stones remind,
Of love divine, of ties that bind.
A pilgrimage that heals the soul,
Transforming fragments to make us whole.

The Wound of Unfulfilled Worship

In silent halls where echoes swell,
We gather here with hearts that dwell.
Upon the altar, hopes once bright,
Now shrouded in the deepest night.

The candles flicker, shadows dance,
Each prayer a wish, a fleeting chance.
Yet empty palms reach to the sky,
Though tears may fall, still we must try.

Oh, wound that festers, deep and raw,
We seek the grace behind the flaw.
To mend the spirit, heal the strife,
In the presence of the sacred life.

Yet still we linger, lost in pain,
As love once vibrant feels like rain.
Each drop a tear, each sigh a song,
In the silence, we fight to belong.

But from the ashes, hope shall rise,
With every wound, a chance to rise.
Through unfulfilled, we seek the true,
In our devotion, we find anew.

Withering Petals on a Stolen Altar

Scattered petals, soft and fair,
Rest upon the altar's prayer.
Each bloom once bright, now faded grace,
Whispers of love, lost in place.

The fragrant scents of yesterday,
Echo the dreams that slipped away.
In tranquil spaces, voices sigh,
As time unravels and flowers die.

With every thrum of a beating heart,
We question where the blessings start.
Is worship more than sights and sounds?
In fading petals, beauty abounds.

Yet in this stillness, hope must find,
The strength within the torn and blind.
To rise and gather what's been lost,
To claim the altar, no matter the cost.

As withering petals breathe their last,
We hold the past, but not fast.
From ashes of grief, new life will grow,
With each sunset, a chance to sow.

Dreams Left at the Temple Gates

At the threshold, where hope collides,
We leave our dreams, where silence hides.
With heavy hearts, we cross this line,
As faith and doubt intertwine.

The gates loom tall, a solemn sight,
Each whispered prayer, a flickering light.
In shadows deep, our yearnings rest,
Grains of desire in a sacred nest.

Oh, dreams abandoned, cast aside,
In the temple's depths, where truths abide.
What once was clear, now draped in mist,
We seek the path our hearts have missed.

And though we leave in search of peace,
The echoes linger, never cease.
In every step, a trace remains,
Of hopes once nurtured, now held in chains.

Yet in this leaving, a promise stirs,
The journey continues, hope reassures.
For dreams may fade, but not erase,
At the gates of faith, we find our place.

The Weight of a Quiet Reprisal

In shadows deep where sorrows dwell,
A whisper floats, a mournful bell.
Each heart, a forge of silent pain,
Bears witness to the quiet reign.

The echoes of what once was bright,
Rest heavy now, a fading light.
Yet in the dusk, hope must arise,
To lift the weight 'neath tempest skies.

Reflecting on the paths we tread,
With choices made and words unsaid.
Each step a prayer, each breath a plea,
For solace found in divine decree.

And through the silence, peace may bloom,
Defying darkness, banishing gloom.
With faith the anchor, steadfast and true,
The quiet reprisal, life anew.

So walk we forth in softened grace,
Embracing love in every space.
For burdens shared, together we bear,
In sacred bond, we find repair.

Unfurling the Veils of Remorse

In twilight's hush, a heart laid bare,
The heavy weight of each despair.
Veils of remorse, like fragile lace,
Conceal the wounds we can't erase.

Yet every tear a story tells,
Of broken dreams in shadowed wells.
We seek redemption in the night,
Unfurling truth towards the light.

The gentle whisper of the soul,
Calls forth the fragments to make whole.
In grace we find the strength to mend,
To journey forth, our spirits blend.

Through valleys deep and mountains high,
With every step, we learn to fly.
Forgiving self, the hardest task,
In quiet moments, truths we ask.

So may we rise from ashes gray,
And hold remorse in love's array.
For in the loss, new paths are drawn,
To greet the dawn with hope reborn.

The Desolate Shrine of Expectation

In silence stands the shrine we raise,
Of hopes entwined in fleeting days.
Expectation, like a whispered prayer,
Etches desire in the air.

But dreams once bright can dim with time,
As shadows creep and life's a climb.
With every promise left unkept,
In our despair, the sorrows crept.

Yet in the dust of what remains,
A flicker glows among the stains.
For every loss, a lesson's gift,
Through broken paths, our spirits lift.

The desolate shrine may seem so bare,
Yet still it breathes a sacred air.
In stillness found, resilience grows,
As faith in whispers gently flows.

So let us honor each chapter penned,
Embrace the twists, the bends, the end.
For every longing, a chance to learn,
In our hearts, the fire shall burn.

When Faith Meets the Specter of Regret

When faith must tread on grounds of loss,
And shadows linger, weary, frost.
Regret, a specter clad in gray,
Haunts the path where we once strayed.

Yet in the darkness, light may shine,
A beacon bright, a sacred sign.
Embrace the weight, the heavy cost,
For every tear is never lost.

In trials faced, we find our way,
Transforming night into the day.
With every falter, lessons take,
The strength to rise, the will to wake.

So gather close, the broken near,
In shared confessions, cast our fear.
For hope can bloom in barren ground,
When kindness sows the seeds we've found.

When faith meets sorrow, hand in hand,
Together we will make our stand.
In every heart, a story grows,
Resilient in the love we chose.

Seraphim Weep for the Untrue

In heavenly realms where light does dwell,
The angels sigh, their sorrow to quell.
Seraphim weep for hearts grown cold,
In pursuit of dreams that tarnish the gold.

A holy chorus, yet silence remains,
For the lost souls bound in their chains.
With wings outspread, they search the night,
For paths of grace, to guide them right.

Soft whispers echo in twilight's embrace,
Calling the lost to redeem their space.
How tender the call, how deep the regret,
To behold the grace that they might forget.

The stars align in celestial tears,
Each drop a prayer for those who are near.
Seraphim weep, but hope still gleams,
In the fractured light of forgotten dreams.

Yet from the ashes, new faith shall rise,
To signal the dawn, to open the skies.
In every heart, a flicker of truth,
Awakens the soul, ignites pure youth.

Dreamt Futures in Ruins

Once we walked in bright, hopeful light,
With visions of peace that felt so right.
But shadows crept, and whispers grew,
Now dreamt futures lie broken in view.

The faith once held has started to fade,
In the ruins of promises silently made.
With every stone, a wish laid bare,
In the rubble of love lies deep despair.

Yet in darkness, a flicker remains,
A soft echo of joy that still claims.
Through trials faced, we must unite,
To build anew in the breaking light.

Hands joined in hope, we softly pray,
For futures reborn from the ashes of gray.
Together we carve what dreams may impart,
As the spirit awakens the weary heart.

Let not the past cast shadows so deep,
For faith's gentle whisper bids us to keep.
Through valleys of sorrow, toward horizons blue,
We rise from the dust to dream strong and true.

Betrayal in the Sanctuary

In the sanctuary where love should reign,
Betrayals linger, a haunting stain.
Whispers of deceit weave through the air,
Silent truths mask a heavy despair.

Once trusted hands now wield the knife,
Innocence pierced, the cost of life.
A place of solace, turned bitter and raw,
Reveals the depths of a forgotten law.

Yet from the ashes, redemption may bloom,
A chance for healing amidst the gloom.
Forgiveness grows where spirits are torn,
A light that shines through the dark, reborn.

Can we mend what has been undone?
In the name of love, let hearts be one.
Though shadows lurk in the corners of grace,
Hope's enduring glow lights the sacred space.

In unity strong, we gather our might,
To banish the dark and restore the light.
For within each soul, lies the power to see,
The beauty of trust, setting spirit free.

Sins of Silence and Woe

In the stillness of night, where shadows creep,
Whispers of sorrow in secrets we keep.
The heart knows the weight of unspoken regret,
For silence breeds wounds that time can't forget.

Each tear that falls bears witness to pain,
A river of sadness, our hidden refrain.
Voices unheard drown in the abyss,
Longing for solace, a moment of bliss.

Yet in the silence, a softness recalls,
The love that can shine through the hardest of walls.
For sins of silence can find their release,
In the warmth of confession, we yearn for peace.

Let us gather our courage, share what we bear,
For hearts entwined can heal with their care.
In the absence of blame, we rise from below,
Together we blossom, as healing can flow.

Boldly we step from the shadows of woe,
With voices united, our spirits aglow.
In the symphony of truth, our souls will sing,
For love is the hope that redemption can bring.

Celestial Shadows on a Fragile Heart

In twilight's glow, the stars do weep,
Shadows dance where secrets creep.
A heart of glass, the world places,
Reflections of divine embraces.

In silence, prayers like whispers rise,
Petals fall from ancient skies.
Fragile dreams in cosmic sway,
Touched by grace, led astray.

Beneath the weight of heaven's tune,
A fragile heart seeks light of moon.
Yet in the dark, a promise waits,
With love that heals, no bitter fates.

Celestial shadows gently guide,
Through valleys deep, where fears reside.
Each heartbeat echoes faith's embrace,
Carving hope in time and space.

In unity, we share the night,
With every star, a thread of light.
With fragile hearts, we learn to stand,
Together swayed by heaven's hand.

Exodus from the Garden of Promises

Once we walked where lilies bloomed,
In soft whispers, dreams were groomed.
With every breath, a sacred space,
Fell from grace, we lost that place.

Temptation's bite, a bitter seed,
In shadows grew, our hearts concede.
We wandered far, from paths so bright,
Seeking solace in endless night.

Yet within our souls, a longing grows,
To find the light where compassion flows.
In exile's grip, we search for part,
The garden's glow within our heart.

Mountains high and valleys wide,
We tread this road, with love our guide.
In echoes soft, the spirit yearns,
To heal the wounds, the world adjourns.

Through trials faced, we gather strength,
In every step, we find our length.
So let the dawn break on the wise,
A new beginning, the soul's reprise.

Requiem for Lost Belief

In the stillness of night's soft breath,
Whispers linger, traces of death.
A silence deep, where hope once stirred,
Now shadows dwell, and dreams are blurred.

Hands clasped in prayer, a fading light,
Glimmers of faith, lost from sight.
Each promise made, now hangs like smoke,
In the void where spirits choke.

Yet amidst the ashes, embers glow,
With trembling hearts, we strive to know.
A requiem for what we've lost,
A path to find our winter frost.

In the depths where sorrows meet,
We seek the warmth, the love's heartbeat.
Voices lifted, a chorus strong,
In unity, we forge along.

Though belief may wane, we still ignite,
With every dawn, we seek the light.
Rebirth from ruin, a soul's refrain,
In every loss, life will remain.

The Wounds of Divine Disappointment

When heavens weep, and sigh with pain,
The heart confesses, its deep disdain.
Heavy burdens, we all must bear,
Wounds of faith, stripped raw and bare.

In sacred texts, we seek the balm,
But echoes resonate, far from calm.
Each tear a testament, a plea for grace,
In silence lost, we search for place.

Divine intentions, we question still,
As shadows linger, against our will.
In struggles faced, the spirits mourn,
A legacy forever worn.

Yet hope persists, a restless seed,
From brokenness, we learn to lead.
Through darkest nights, we forge ahead,
With love as guide, we brave the dread.

For every wound, a lesson gleaned,
In pain, the soul's bright essence dreamed.
Disappointment fades, as light breaks free,
In every crack, new clarity.

The Last Supper of Broken Beliefs

In shadows dim where faith once stood,
We gather 'round the table of wood.
The bread once shared now crumbles slow,
The wine is bitter, the truth laid low.

Voices echo in the hollow night,
Silent prayers seek the fading light.
Sins revealed in fragile grace,
Together we mourn this sacred space.

The hands we raised in fervent prayer,
Now tremble in our deep despair.
The promise made, a dream's soft sigh,
Transformed to whispers as hopes die.

Yet in the silence, love endures,
A flicker of faith that still reassures.
Through broken vows and fading yearn,
In heart's deep ache, we still discern.

So let us drink to what remains,
The bond that ties through all the pains.
For in this loss, a lesson grows,
In darkest nights, the spirit glows.

Lillys Blooming from Ashes

From soot and dust, the flowers rise,
With tender grace 'neath open skies.
Each petal soft, a tale of woe,
Yet in their beauty, hope does grow.

In gardens bright where shadows dwell,
The lilly speaks of dreams once fell.
Though trials harsh have left their scars,
They reach for light, they seek the stars.

The ashes cling, a memory's weight,
Yet blooms emerge to celebrate.
In every heart, resilience springs,
A melody that life still sings.

Through seasons cold, the spirit fights,
To turn the dark to radiant lights.
In every bruise, a story spun,
Of rising strong when day is done.

Let lilies flourish, let hope renew,
For in their strength, the world shines through.
In grief's embrace, we find our way,
From ashes blooms a brand new day.

The Weight of a Fallen Angel's Wing

Beneath the heavens where angels tread,
One fell softly, its light now shed.
With feathered grace turned into stone,
It carries burdens, deep and alone.

Each rustle whispers of a tale untold,
Of dreams that faded, of hearts turned cold.
The weight of sorrow now lingers near,
An echo of love turned to silent fear.

In twilight's grace, the shadows bend,
And hopes once high now struggle to mend.
A fallen angel, a mournful sight,
Yet even here, a flicker of light.

Though wings may drag through the heavy night,
In darkness found, there lies a fight.
For through the pain, redemption waits,
A chance to soar beyond the gates.

So bear the weight, embrace the fall,
For in each struggle, we hear the call.
To rise again with strength anew,
A testament to all we've been through.

Shattered Vows in Sacred Light

In sacred halls where whispers fade,
Our vows once bright now feel betrayed.
The light that shone through promised grace,
Now fractures in this hollow space.

With trembling hands, we trace the lines,
Each broken word, each fault defined.
Yet in the cracks, a glimmer glows,
A fragile hope that slowly grows.

In unity once, our hearts aligned,
Now scattered dreams, our souls unwind.
Yet love persists through veils of pain,
In every loss, we still remain.

Through shadows thick, we search for peace,
In shattered vows, we find release.
For even in despair's cruel clutch,
The bonds we've forged still linger much.

So let us walk this path of plight,
To mend the wounds with sacred light.
For every tear, a lesson learned,
In shattered vows, new hope returned.

Echoes of the Unkept Covenant

In shadows deep, the promise fades,
A sacred vow, where light invades.
The trembling hearts in silence weep,
For broken bonds, our souls to keep.

The rain descends, a gentle sigh,
While spirits mourn, and angels cry.
The words once spoke, now linger low,
In chambers where the lost ones go.

Beneath the stars, the night reveals,
Our fragile faith, the unrest feels.
We seek the truth, but shadows part,
In hollow echoes of the heart.

The altar stands, adorned in dust,
A relic born of shattered trust.
Yet whispers float on evening's breath,
Reminding us of love and death.

Across the fields, the spirits roam,
In search of grace, in search of home.
We walk the path, though darkness grows,
In echoes of the unkept throes.

Fractured Benedictions

Beneath the steeple, prayers collide,
The fractured notes where hope resides.
In whispered tones, the faithful plead,
As mercy waits on humankind's need.

The candles flicker, shadows dance,
In sacred spaces, we take a chance.
Our hearts laid bare, the burdens shared,
To bind the wounds we've deep declared.

The hymns of old, now worn and thin,
Resound the cries of where we've been.
Yet through the dark, a light persists,
In fractured benedictions, we exist.

The echoes fade in empty halls,
As silence speaks, and darkness calls.
We seek the bonds that once were strong,
In fractured paths, we still belong.

To grasp the light, the love once known,
Amidst the thorns, a seed is sown.
With every prayer, our souls align,
In fractured benedictions, we find divine.

The Forsaken Altar

In twilight's grasp, the altar stands,
Once filled with gifts from faithful hands.
Now echoes linger, ghosts of prayer,
In silence deep, our hearts laid bare.

The incense rises, memories swirl,
Where once was peace, now chaos unfurl.
We search for solace in the night,
Yet find only shadows in our plight.

With broken idols, dust and grief,
We yearn for love, a deep relief.
In every tear, a tale unfolds,
Of sacrifices, and stories told.

The altar waits, with arms spread wide,
For wandering souls who turn and guide.
In every whisper, a chance to mend,
The forsaken altar, our hearts' true friend.

In candle's glow, we find our way,
Through hollow echoes of yesterday.
We bend our knees, our hopes awake,
At the forsaken altar, love's retake.

Lost in the Whispered Confessions

In dim-lit rooms, where shadows creep,
We share our fears, our secrets deep.
Each whispered breath, a fragile thread,
Connecting souls where angels tread.

The night unfolds, our hearts laid bare,
In whispered tones, we find our prayer.
The burdens shift, relinquished sighs,
As shadows dance beneath the skies.

The light slips in, a soft embrace,
In quiet corners, we seek grace.
With every story, healing starts,
In whispered confessions, mending hearts.

The echoes linger, truths declared,
In moments tender, souls ensnared.
We walk the path of love's intention,
Lost in the whispered confessions.

Through trials faced, the ties grow strong,
In darkest nights, we find the song.
With voices lifted, spirits soar,
Lost in the whispers, forevermore.

Chasing Shadows of a Lost Benediction

In twilight's glow, the whispers blend,
Silent prayers for a guiding friend.
With every breath, the shadows rise,
Chasing solace in the endless skies.

A benediction, drifting far,
Like echoes clinging to a distant star.
In search of peace, we tread the night,
Through tangled paths, we seek the light.

Yet in the silence, echoes call,
A haunting hymn that stirs the soul.
Within our hearts, a flame remains,
Flickering softly through joy and pains.

Each moment counts, a fleeting chance,
To find our way in life's great dance.
Though shadows loom, we find our grace,
In every challenge, a sacred space.

The Strain of a Frayed Covenant

In the fabric worn, the threads unwind,
A covenant forged, now hard to find.
Promises whispered in solemn tone,
Yet remnants of faith often feel alone.

Through trials faced, with spirits torn,
The heartache woven, though hope is worn.
Yet in the strain, a lesson grows,
Forgiveness blooms where love bestows.

Each tear that falls, a sacred gift,
In shadows cast, the spirits lift.
For in the frayed, we learn to trust,
In broken bonds, we find what's just.

So gather strength from scars we bear,
For in the struggle, we find repair.
With love renewed, the ties restore,
A frayed covenant, yet worth much more.

Memories Etched in Parchment Tears

In every tear, a story flows,
Etched in parchment where the heart knows.
Moments cherished, both joy and strife,
Carved in silence, they shape our life.

With ink of faith, we write our years,
In whispers soft, through laughter and fears.
The sacred bond, a timeless thread,
Connecting hearts, where angels tread.

In memories vast, the shadows dwell,
A tapestry woven, with tales to tell.
Through every loss, love's grace appears,
In cherished moments, through parchment tears.

Though seasons change and time may pass,
Each memory blooms like dew on grass.
For in our hearts, the stories live,
With every tear, we learn to forgive.

The Crossroads of Faith and Despair

At twilight's gate, the crossroads call,
Where faith stands tall, yet fears enthrall.
With trembling hearts, we seek the way,
In shadows deep, we learn to pray.

As darkness looms, doubts fill the air,
Yet flickers of hope weave through despair.
In fervent cries and silent pleas,
We find our strength, our minds find ease.

Though storms may rage and tempests shout,
Within our souls, we search without.
The light that flickers is ever near,
A beacon bright amidst our fear.

So step with care, and lift your gaze,
For at the crossroads, love will blaze.
Through faith and grace, we'll find our path,
In the union of joy, despair shall pass.

Foundations of Trust Crumbling

In shadows where our faith once grew,
The stones have shifted, cracked anew.
Whispers of promise drift away,
Leaving us lost, in disarray.

Once strong and steadfast, now they break,
The light we held begins to quake.
Silent prayers cast to the night,
Yearning for solace, seeking light.

Beneath the weight of doubt we stand,
Grasping the remnants of shifting sand.
The bonds that tethered heart and soul,
Fractured fragments take their toll.

Gaze upon the ruins of our trust,
Each brick a shadow, turned to dust.
In the silence, echoes remain,
A haunting hymn of lost refrain.

Yet in despair, a seed we sow,
For trust may falter, yet still grow.
With faith reborn, we rise again,
To seek the light where hope begins.

A Testament to Vanished Faith

What once was bright now fades away,
A testament to faith's decay.
In holy spaces where we prayed,
The whispers of the lost have strayed.

Lost in the echoes of despair,
Our hearts once filled with fervent care.
Each promise made, now veiled in night,
A distant star, devoid of light.

Shadows stretch where hope once shone,
Grief lays claim to all we've known.
The sacred texts now gather dust,
As words of comfort turn to rust.

In quiet corners, doubts confide,
The empty vessels left inside.
Yet still we search for signs above,
To heal the wounds, to feel the love.

Remember, weary soul, the spark,
Within the darkness, ignites a mark.
Though faith may falter, hope will rise,
To find the light in endless skies.

Sacred Bonds Unraveled

Threads once woven, tightly bound,
Now frayed and drifting, lost, unground.
What sacred pact did we betray?
In silence, sacred words decay.

Cherished oaths lay scattered wide,
No longer held, no longer tried.
The hearts we vowed to keep as one,
Now beat apart, and love's undone.

In moments shared, the laughter fades,
Each promise broken, joy cascades.
A tapestry of dreams unspooled,
Where once we danced, now pain has ruled.

We search for meaning in the void,
Where once our faith, now love destroyed.
In battles lost, we learn to heal,
To weave anew, our hearts to seal.

May wisdom grow from our despair,
For bonds can mend, with tender care.
In time, the threads may yet renew,
And flow with grace, as love breaks through.

The Parable of Forsaken Pledges

In tales of old, the burdens shared,
A parable of trust laid bare.
The promises, like morning dew,
Once bright, now fade, this truth rings true.

Faithful vows made under starry skies,
Now slip away like whispered sighs.
The stories told, now lie in dust,
As hope gives way to silent rust.

Once we walked upon sacred ground,
In unity, our hearts were found.
But time has threaded doubt through words,
And love retreats like startled birds.

Yet through the tears, a lesson learned,
To seek the light where faith has burned.
For in the ashes, hope ignites,
And turns our fears to sacred rites.

Embrace the scars that mark the past,
For from the ruins, love can last.
In every heart, a chance to grow,
To bind our spirits, let love flow.

Surrendered Hopes on the Sacred Trail

In the stillness of the night, I stand,
With weary heart and trembling hand.
Each step I take, a prayer I weave,
On sacred paths, I learn to believe.

The stars above, like whispers bright,
Guide me through the shadowed light.
In surrender, my spirit finds grace,
In silence, I seek Your holy face.

For every burden that I bear,
I lay it down in fervent prayer.
With every sigh, a hope released,
In Your embrace, my soul finds peace.

The trail is long, the journey vast,
Yet in Your love, I anchor fast.
Through trials faced and mountains high,
I know with You, I cannot die.

With faith as my shield, I walk ahead,
In every tear, the joy is spread.
For on this path, hope is reborn,
A sacred trust, in You, I mourn.

Remnants of the Divine Exchange

In the quiet of the evening glow,
I ponder each moment, the ebb and flow.
What once was filled now stands so bare,
A tapestry worn, threads of despair.

Yet in these remnants, whispers call,
Of grace bestowed, beyond the fall.
The divine exchange, a holy quest,
In giving, I find a heartbeat's rest.

Fragments of mercy, scattered wide,
Echoing stories where souls abide.
In every struggle, a lesson learned,
In sharing love, the heart is turned.

The dust of earth, the spark divine,
Intertwined in every line.
Through shadows deep, Your light will shine,
In surrendered hope, life's love aligns.

As remnants fade, the spirit soars,
With open hands, I seek Your doors.
In every breath, I find a way,
To cherish the remnants of yesterday.

Withering Hopes in a Harvest of Ashes

In fields once rich, where dreams took flight,
Now lay the echoes of lost light.
Withering hopes, like autumn leaves,
Fallen to ground, the heart deceives.

The harvest's yield, a bitter taste,
What once was plenty now lies waste.
Yet from the ashes, new seeds can grow,
With faith's embrace, life starts to flow.

In sorrow's grip, I kneel and pray,
For dawn to break, to light the way.
In every tear, a story spun,
Yet from the dark, behold the sun.

For even in loss, Your love remains,
In all the grief, eternal gains.
With every trial, a lesson given,
In hope renewed, my soul is risen.

Withering hopes, a place to mend,
In sacred ashes, I shall transcend.
From despair's clutch, my spirit will rise,
In the harvest of hope, my heart defies.

The Shimmer of Promises Gone Awry

In twilight's glow, the shadows play,
Where promises made have slipped away.
The shimmer dims in evening's sigh,
Yet still I seek the reasons why.

What once was clear now fades to gray,
In broken dreams, I find my way.
A journey marked by starlit doubt,
Each step I take, I hear Your shout.

With every tarnished hope, I learn,
Through all the pain, my spirit yearns.
In ashes cold, the fire ignites,
In darkness deep, Your love invites.

Though promises wane like evening's breath,
In every loss, there lies a depth.
A shimmer still, amidst the plight,
In faith's embrace, I find the light.

For even when all seems to stray,
Your guiding hand will lead the way.
In every tear, a grace bestowed,
In trust renewed, our hearts are sowed.

In the Shadow of a Fading Promise

In twilight's veil, where shadows grow,
The whispers of hope begin to slow.
Yet in the darkness, faith still shines,
A flicker of love in sacred signs.

Beneath the weight of old despair,
We seek the light, we lift our prayer.
For even lost, the heart will yearn,
In every trial, our souls will burn.

The promise once bright, now dulled by night,
Yet embers glow with fervent might.
Through valleys deep, our spirits run,
In search of grace, till day is won.

With every doubt, a seed of trust,
In broken dreams, we find what's just.
Though futures dim, the past still sings,
Of joy reborn in hidden springs.

So let us walk in patient grace,
Embracing love in every space.
For promises lost can still be found,
In gentle whispers that resound.

Unraveling the Divine Thread

In the tapestry of life unspooled,
Each strand a story, divinely ruled.
We wander paths of chance and fate,
In woven hearts, we dare to wait.

The fabric pure with colors bright,
Is threaded through with sacred light.
In every knot where troubles weave,
A testament of love we believe.

Through trials faced and burdens borne,
The thread of faith keeps us adorned.
For in the fray, our spirits blend,
In every loss, we find a friend.

As patterns shift and shadows play,
We learn to trust in the Divine Way.
Each twist and turn, a lesson learned,
In every heart, the fire burned.

So let us hold this tapestry,
With threads of hope, we set them free.
In unity, we comprehend,
The grace that flows, without an end.

Echoes of Grace in Dismay

In shadows cast by endless night,
The echoes of grace bring forth the light.
In quiet corners, spirits sigh,
Yet in their ache, still seek the sky.

For every tear that falls like rain,
A whisper comes to ease the pain.
In dismay's grip, we yearn to find,
The gentle touch of love unconfined.

Amidst the storm, our faith holds fast,
In trials faced, we are unsurpassed.
For grace ignites our weary souls,
Restoring hope and making whole.

Through every heart that feels alone,
A symphony sings, a sacred tone.
In disarray, we hear the call,
To rise in love, to stand, not fall.

So in our trials, let grace unfold,
Sustaining warmth when days are cold.
In echoes soft, the promise stays,
With every breath, we sing His praise.

The Penitent Heart's Gentle Cry

In silence deep, a heart will pine,
For mercy pure, for love divine.
Each tear a token, each sigh a plea,
In aching souls, we long to be free.

With every misstep, burdens grow,
Yet in repentance, grace will flow.
In humble prayer, we seek the light,
To guide us onward through the night.

For every fear that clouds the mind,
In penance sweet, true peace we find.
The gentle cry of souls laid bare,
Invokes a love beyond compare.

Though paths may twist, and shadows stretch,
In heartfelt cries, our souls connect.
A journey wild, yet tenderly led,
In every heartbeat, faith is fed.

So let us kneel with hearts so bare,
In whispered hopes, our earnest prayer.
For in the dark, we find the grace,
To love anew, to seek His face.

Shattered Vows of the Faithful

In the silence of night, promises fade,
Hearts once entwined, now they evade.
All the prayers whispered, lost in the breeze,
Echoes of love, now brought to their knees.

Covenants crafted under heaven's grace,
Frayed by the storms that time can't erase.
Faith once a fortress, now merely a ghost,
What was once cherished, now seldom discussed.

Lifetimes spent building a bright, shared dream,
Now scattered like ashes, lost in the stream.
The altar stands empty, adorned with despair,
Faithful hearts yearning for moments to share.

In shadows they wander, seeking the light,
Searching for solace in the depths of the night.
Yet hope lingers softly within every soul,
A spark in the darkness, it calls them back whole.

Beneath the starlit sky, they lift their gaze,
To find redemption in the prayerful ways.
Though shattered, their vows still whisper the past,
In love's tender grace, they long to hold fast.

Covenant Fragments Beneath the Stars

Under the vastness, the silence grows loud,
Fragments of vows hide within the crowd.
Promises shattered, scattered like seas,
Mending the heart is not done with ease.

Whispers of old haunt the cool desert air,
Love that was fervent, but turned into prayer.
Covenants starlit in the tapestry weave,
Broken connections that cleave as they grieve.

Each shared glance once a sacred exchange,
Now a reminder of love that feels strange.
Beneath the heavens, they kneel to implore,
Restoration of trust, to be lost evermore.

In the stillness echoes stories untold,
Hearts of the faithful feel weary and cold.
Yet beneath the stars, a flicker remains,
The hope of revival amidst all the pains.

With faith as their lantern, they seek the divine,
For healing to enter these hearts once entwined.
Though fragments remain from the definitions carved,
Dreams of togetherness still feel preserved.

Whispers of Lost Commitments

In the shadows of doubt, time holds its breath,
Vows once eternal now waltz with death.
Softly, the murmurs of promises fade,
A tapestry unraveling, faith frayed.

Once vibrant colors now washed in despair,
Commitments once sacred drift in the air.
Hands once united in fervent embrace,
Now tremble in silence, in sorrow they face.

Lost in the echoes of what could have been,
Hearts wander alone, seeking solace within.
Each tear like a prayer, a plea to the skies,
For love to return, for truth to arise.

Yet there in the darkness, a glimmer appears,
A chance for revival, a silencing of fears.
From whispers of loss, new beginnings take flight,
Restoration awaits in the calm of the night.

With faith as their guide, they journey anew,
Piecing together the faithfulness true.
For every commitment may bend, but not break,
The heart's gentle rhythm still yearns to awake.

Sanctity Torn Asunder

Under the weight of forgotten decree,
Sanctity crumbles, just shadows will be.
Fractured foundations of bonds that were strong,
Now echo with sorrow, a melancholic song.

Prayers once spoken in fervor and grace,
Meet silence now met with a hollowed space.
Echoing heartbeats, a rhythm of pain,
Longing for peace that won't come back again.

The altar stands solemn, with hearts filled with dread,
Where laughter once lingered, now silence is fed.
A covenant's promise, once light as the air,
Now shrouded in whispers of memories laid bare.

Yet deep in the fractures, a longing still glows,
For hope to return where the river once flows.
Though torn is the fabric, the stitches can mend,
With faith as the needle, the journey won't end.

In the depths of surrender, they kneel and they plead,
For sanctity born from the ruins to lead.
For love that's been battered can rise from the dust,
Restoring the spirits, rekindling the trust.

Portraits of Fissured Trust

In shadows where belief once gleamed,
Fissures crack the sacred seam.
Voices murmur, hearts remain,
Trust now dances with our pain.

Whispers echo, doubts arise,
Promises caught in azure skies.
Yet among the cracks, lights break through,
A tapestry of faith renewed.

Hands once clasped in fervent prayer,
Now tremble in the open air.
Yet still we search for guiding light,
In the silence of the night.

Hope lingers in the back of minds,
As we seek what truth unwinds.
Each heart a sanctuary frail,
Bound by love, yet bruised and pale.

In the fissures, grace can flow,
A chance to heal what we let go.
In broken trust, we find our way,
To a dawn that lights the day.

A Journey through Sacred Doubt

Amidst the path where shadows tread,
Sacred doubt weaves tales unsaid.
Hearts adorned with fragile trust,
Wander forth, as pilgrims must.

Questions linger in the air,
Desires echo, silent prayers.
Searching souls in twilight's grace,
Find their footprints in this space.

Winds of change will lift the veil,
Yet storms of doubt may seek to prevail.
With each stumble, understanding grows,
In the heart where faith still glows.

Turning towards the sacred flame,
Seeking comfort, none the same.
In this journey, we embrace,
The divine within the chase.

Each step, a whisper on the earth,
Guides us through the trials of worth.
Together we tread this sacred ground,
In holy doubts, our strength is found.

The Remnants of Celestial Vows

In starlit night, we make our plea,
Celestial vows, so wild and free.
Yet time unravels threads once spun,
Leaves us wondering what's been done.

Promises echo with fading light,
In remnants strong, we seek our sight.
Each vow a seed in the soil of dreams,
Waiting for love's gentle beams.

Hearts that weep in silent grace,
Long for signs in empty space.
Yet within each shard of past,
Is hope that rises, firm and vast.

Let us gather, stitch by stitch,
Mending faith without a hitch.
In the tapestry of our design,
Celestial threads will intertwine.

Though shadows loom and doubts bespeak,
In our hearts, love still will seek.
The remnants strong, forever thrive,
In celestial promises, we revive.

Beneath the Weight of Unyielding Expectation

Beneath the weight, we wander slow,
Unyielding tides of what we owe.
Each heartbeat echoes dreams once dreamed,
In silent prayers, our spirits beamed.

Expectations, like towering walls,
Press against us as darkness falls.
Yet within the depths of fear,
Compassion breathes and draws us near.

In struggles fierce, we find our voice,
To question, ponder, and rejoice.
For unyielding paths may bend and sway,
Yet love will guide us on our way.

From burdens heavy, we shall rise,
And cast our hopes beyond the skies.
In unity, we face the storm,
For in our hearts, we are reborn.

Together, hand in hand we soar,
Embracing life, forevermore.
Beneath the weight of doubt and strife,
We find the essence of our life.

Corrupted Allegiance in the Light

In the glow of promise bright,
Hearts once pure now tremble slight,
Whispers lure them from the path,
Tempting shadows, kindled wrath.

Fingers trace the fading scroll,
Scripture lost, unholy toll,
Betrayed by those who claim to see,
In the depth of a hollow decree.

Faith erodes in silent night,
Boundless grace turned into blight,
Eyes that wander, souls that stray,
Corrupted dreams lead hearts away.

In the skies an echo rings,
Calling back the wayward flings,
Yet the fervor dims in shade,
Hope's embrace now feels afraid.

Come forth, ye pilgrims of the light,
Seek the truth, reclaim the right,
In the conflict, nurture prayer,
For in the seeking, find the rare.

A Psalter of Fractured Faith

Voices sing in fractured chords,
Melodies of waning words,
Scriptures torn, yet still they plead,
Yearning hearts, a sacred need.

Among the ruins, shadows creep,
Psalters sung, yet hearts they keep,
Beneath the weight of shattered trust,
In each silence, chaos rusts.

Wounds of faith once deeply sown,
Blossoms bloom in seeds alone,
Hope, like grain, withers to dust,
Yet within, the ember's thrust.

Sacred texts with echoes ring,
Burdens shared, the pain they bring,
In the gathering dusk, we stand,
Holding tightly to His hand.

When the dawn of new grace dawns,
Fractured faith still carries on,
Every note, a prayer, a plea,
Harmony finds a way to be.

The Martyrdom of Unrealized Hopes

In the valley where dreams die,
Silent screams, a mournful sigh,
Unrealized, hopes lie in wait,
Each heartbeat seals a fate.

Promises like flickers fade,
Martyr's path, a heavy grade,
Beneath the burden, lost ideals,
Wounds that time can never heal.

Faithful hearts in shadows roam,
Yearn for light to call them home,
Yet the horizon's shrouded view,
Hides the glory, hides the true.

In the gloom, their voices rise,
Echoed hopes touch the skies,
Each lament a testament,
Bearing grief, a life well spent.

Through the struggle, spirits soar,
Martyrs seeking evermore,
Each tear a prayer, softly told,
In the silence, faith grows bold.

Temptation of the Unrealized Wish

Whispers weave through the still night,
Tempting hearts from the divine light,
Unrealized wishes take their hold,
In the shadows, secrets unfold.

Promises glimmer like distant stars,
Yearning souls bear unseen scars,
Each desire, a fleeting breeze,
Caught in webs of false decease.

Faith retreats with the rising tide,
Unrealized dreams, nowhere to bide,
In the chase, the spirit bends,
Craving solace that never ends.

Yet amidst the yearning void,
Wisdom waits, the heart deployed,
True fulfillment in surrender lies,
In letting go, the spirit flies.

Temptations fade in sacred trust,
Wishes grounded, rise from dust,
Tread the path where blessings flow,
In the heart, true riches glow.

The Silence between the Prayers

In the hushed dawn, voices fade,
Hearts whisper softly, feeling betrayed.
Hope hangs heavy, like dew on the grass,
In silence, the moments quietly pass.

Each word a droplet of faith's pure plea,
Yet stillness reigns where hearts long to be.
The echoes linger, a haunting refrain,
In silence, we bear our unspoken pain.

Beneath the weight of devotion's still night,
We seek the lost warmth, the spirit's light.
In sacred communion, we gather alone,
In silence, the whispers are softly intoned.

With trembling hands, we raise our hearts high,
Yet find no answer to every sigh.
In the cradle of silence, belief starts to fray,
A longing for solace that slips away.

The silence between us, a chasm so wide,
In the space of our prayers, where shadows abide.
Yet somewhere in stillness, a promise does wait,
In the folds of the silence, we still contemplate.

A Binding That Betrayed the Soul

In shadows we wandered, hand in hand,
Chained by the whispers of fate's cruel strand.
Each promise a thread, once woven with care,
Now frayed and tangled in burdens we bear.

What binding adorned this fragile heart?
A tapestry torn, where the edges depart.
In faith's solemn vow, there came a cruel twist,
A heart once so certain, now lost in the mist.

Oh, what a journey, this maze we've embraced,
With bonds that we trusted, now laced with disgrace.
In the quiet of night, betrayal unveils,
A binding that crippled, where hope slowly pales.

Yet in the darkness, a flicker remains,
A whisper of grace beneath all the chains.
For even in sorrow, a lesson unfolds,
The soul's silent strength is worth more than gold.

Through trials we walk, in anguish we strive,
In the depths of despair, we begin to revive.
What once felt like shackles, we learn to renew,
A binding transformed, as the spirit breaks through.

Candlelight Flickers, Faith Withers

In shadows of twilight, the candles burn low,
A flicker of hope in the soft evening glow.
Each flame tells a story of dreams left untold,
As faith dances softly, flickering bold.

Yet with every breath, the air feels so thin,
A whisper of doubt begins to creep in.
As candlelight wanes, shadows stretch long,
In the heart of the night, where faith feels so wrong.

What once was a blaze now struggles to stand,
As flickering embers slip through our hands.
In moments of stillness, the heart starts to tire,
As doubts cast their shadows, consuming the fire.

Yet amidst the darkness, a glimmer remains,
For even dim flickers can soften the chains.
Though faith may wither, it learns to ignite,
In the warmth of the struggle, we find our true light.

So let the candles flicker, let shadows take flight,
For even in darkness, there's a push towards light.
With each quiet prayer, and each silent plea,
The soul finds its strength, and begins to break free.

The Echo of Unanswered Devotion

In the sacred stillness, we gather in prayer,
A longing for solace, a hope to share.
Yet silence envelops the fervent heart's call,
The echo of longing, a silence that falls.

We lift up our voices with passion and grace,
But what of the answers that life can't replace?
In the depths of our yearning, confusion takes hold,
An echo of love that feels distant and cold.

Each prayer a reflection, a mirror of doubt,
In the depths of the soul, where faith wears out.
Yet still in the quiet, a whisper is known,
The echo of devotion, though unanswered, has grown.

For within the void, a strength we must find,
A testament written in the heart and the mind.
Even when voices are lost in the haze,
The echo of grace still sings in the praise.

In the shadows of night, or the light of the day,
The echo of love never fades away.
Though answers we seek may evade our intent,
The spirit remembers what devotion has sent.

Adrift in the Sea of Quiet Reproach

In stillness, shadows linger near,
Whispers echo, drawing fear.
Wave upon wave of thoughts collide,
Lost in waters, nowhere to hide.

A lighthouse glimmers in the night,
Guiding hearts towards the light.
Yet doubts crash like storms untamed,
In the silence, souls are blamed.

Hope once glimmered in the dawn,
Fading fast, now almost gone.
Yet love's embrace holds tight my stance,
In the depths, I'll still take a chance.

With every tide, my spirit sways,
Seeking solace in secret ways.
Though reproach may haunt my heart,
In faith, I'll find a brand new start.

Adrift, I'll navigate my course,
Held by grace, my inner force.
For in the quiet, truth will find,
A beacon shining, ever kind.

Veils of Deception in Sacred Spaces

Beneath the arches, shadows play,
Whispers dance where truth goes astray.
Veils of fabric, pure yet worn,
Hide the scars of hearts that mourn.

In hushed tones, the faithful speak,
Beneath their strength, their spirits weak.
Masks of virtue conceal the lie,
In sacred halls, the silent cry.

Light flickers, casting doubt all around,
Lost in echoes, no solace found.
Yet amidst the veils, a glimmer appears,
Hope arising, dissolving fears.

They gather in prayer, hands intertwined,
Seeking truth, yet often blind.
A call for honesty starts to spark,
To tear away the deceptive dark.

Within these walls, hearts intertwine,
Longing for a love divine.
With each layer of falsehood shed,
The light of grace will be widespread.

God's Heartbeat in the Fracture

In every crack, a whispered prayer,
God's heartbeat softens the despair.
When life shatters, pieces strewn,
In brokenness, a sacred tune.

The pulse of love, a healing song,
In the depths where the lost belong.
Fractured souls find a way to mend,
In the chaos, we learn to bend.

Through trials faced, hearts intertwined,
In darkness, a light defined.
When hope is thin, and faith feels weak,
God's presence comforts, breathes, and speaks.

The fractures tell of journeys made,
The strength in weakness, love displayed.
With every heart that learns to break,
God's heartbeat offers a way to wake.

So in the fractures, let us see,
God's love flows like a gentle sea.
Embrace the broken, trust the art,
For in the fracture, lies the heart.

In the Wake of the Unfulfilled

Dreams once bright, now whisper low,
In the wake of hopes, we learn to grow.
Time passes like a fleeting breath,
In the unfulfilled, we confront death.

Promises made linger in air,
Echoes of love, shadows of care.
Yet every loss births a new way,
To find the light in a lingering gray.

Through every ache, a lesson learned,
In the ashes, a fire burned.
What seemed lost may yet arise,
From the depths, a new sunrise.

Hold tight to dreams that still remain,
In the struggle, embrace the pain.
For in the wake of unfulfilled song,
We'll find the paths where we belong.

With every heartbeat, let us stand,
In the wake, we'll hold God's hand.
Through trials faced, the spirit thrives,
In the unfulfilled, true meaning arrives.

Trust Torn in the Name of Grace

In shadows deep where faith wanes,
A heart exposed, confronted with chains.
Whispers of doubt vex the soul,
Yet still we search for the whole.

In grace we falter, in trust we break,
A mirror cracked, reflecting our ache.
The light we seek, so hard to embrace,
As storms of despair cloud our grace.

Yet hope like a flower, pushes through stone,
In barren fields, our spirits have grown.
To trust again, the fragile must rise,
With open hearts, to touch the skies.

Belief rekindles beneath silent plea,
In the heart's quiet chambers, we find we are free.
The torn threads weave a tapestry bright,
Restoring the faith lost in the night.

So gather the pieces, lay them in prayer,
For trust, once broken, can still be laid bare.
In grace, we find solace, a shimmering lace,
And hope is reborn in the name of grace.

The Sins of a Hollow Testament

Upon the altar, words softly spoken,
Yet hollow echoes leave spirits broken.
The sins we harbor, the lines we draw,
Depict a faith that stirs not a flaw.

With pages worn and tales untold,
Lies a truth that silently unfolds.
The testament frail in the hands of doubt,
Forging a path we cannot live without.

In rituals blind, we seek to atone,
Yet grasping shadows, we stand alone.
The cries of mercy hang in the air,
But the heart knows well this weight of despair.

We wander through lessons, blind to their grace,
For sin and surrender wear a strange face.
In hollow tomes, the spirit convicts,
In search of redemption, our hearts contradict.

Yet still we rise, embers in dark,
As the spark of faith ignites a new arc.
In the sins we confess, the truth lays bare,
The hollow testament, a bridge to repair.

Adrift in Divine Disappointment

On waves of longing, we drift and sway,
Seeking the light that has gone astray.
In solemnity's grasp, our hopes do float,
Yet silence remains, a frigid moat.

We reach for heaven, yet grasp at air,
Our prayers, like feathers, dissolve in despair.
In the depths of yearning, we wrestle and moan,
Adrift in visions, we feel so alone.

The promise of grace hangs just out of reach,
In moments of doubt, it's hard to beseech.
Yet somewhere beneath the turmoil and tides,
A whisper of love continuously guides.

A flicker of hope in the stormy sea,
As faith wades out and invites us to be.
Though trials come hard, and visions may crack,
We find in the struggle, a path to unpack.

For adrift we may feel, yet shores are in sight,
In the dance of the waves, we claim our birthright.
With prayers like anchors, we navigate fear,
In divine disappointment, love always draws near.

Celestial Promises, Earthly Failures

In starry skies, the promises gleam,
Yet on this earth, we lose our dream.
Celestial whispers fall soft like rain,
Still hearts are heavy, must bear the strain.

For every promise, a shadow appears,
With earthly burdens and unwept tears.
The distance between is a chasm wide,
In longing for solace, we oft must abide.

As moonlight dances on restless seas,
We search for answers, yet often freeze.
Amidst the failures, redemption stands tall,
In grace we falter, in mercy we call.

Yet hope remains, like a star burning bright,
Guiding the lost through the thick of night.
Celestial promises in our hearts take flight,
To mends the fractures and ignite the light.

So walk we must on this path of strife,
With faith as our anchor, we cherish our life.
Though earthly failures might cloud our array,
Celestial promises will light our way.

When the Altar Fell Silent

When the altar fell silent, hearts did mourn,
Whispers of faith replaced by the scorn.
Candles flickered dim in the dark,
Doubts swallowed the light, left no spark.

Sinners would gather, seeking the grace,
Yet found only shadows, a hollowed space.
The voices of angels drifted away,
Leaving behind what they couldn't betray.

In the stillness, prayers were unheard,
Each soul felt heavy, broken and blurred.
Fingers clasped tight, in trembling resolve,
Yearning for answers the heart can absolve.

A murmur of hope broke the long night,
Each heart lifted gently towards the light.
When the altar fell silent, love still stood,
Waiting to gather the lost like a flood.

And as dawn approached, soft and divine,
Faith once abandoned began to align.
From the ashes of silence, a new song rose,
In the hearts of the faithful, love ever glows.

Echoes of Unkept Oaths

In the shadows of prayers, oaths lay bare,
Promises spoken with a heart laid to share.
Yet time stole the breath of those sacred vows,
Leaving the faithful to question and browse.

Whispers of hope lingered like smoke,
Each echo of laughter a heart's cruel joke.
Wounds from the past still bleed in the night,
Unkept oaths haunt like phantoms in flight.

Did the heavens weep when silence took hold?
Did the angels forsake the fervent and bold?
In dreams they would falter, in daylight retreat,
Wishing for strength, yet tasting defeat.

Yet still in the dark, glimmers of light,
Reviving the souls that yearn for the right.
In the depths of their sorrow, resolve is reformed,
From the ruins of oaths, a new faith is born.

As the echoes fade softly from their plea,
The heart learns to chant its own melody.
For the truest of vows are those forged in pain,
Echoes of unkept oaths, now wisdom gained.

The Penance of Mended Hearts

In the quiet confession, the heart finds its way,
Mended in pieces, learning to pray.
Each tear that fell nurtured the ground,
In the garden of mercy, healing was found.

The weight of the world rests heavy and deep,
Promises broken, secrets to keep.
Yet grace is a river, flowing so free,
Washing the wounds that no eye can see.

Forgiveness a journey, not just a word,
In the chorus of sorrow, redemption is heard.
The penance of mended hearts ever so bright,
Turns the darkest of moments into brilliant light.

With hands open wide to receive the embrace,
They gather their courage, they seek their own place.
In the warmth of compassion, where love reigns true,
Mended hearts flourish, reflecting the view.

So let us remember the power of grace,
In the depths of our trials, find a safe space.
For the journey of healing is sacred and bold,
In the penance of mended hearts, life unfolds.

Prayers Forgotten in the Dark

In the stillness of night, where shadows play sly,
Prayers forgotten in dark whisper and sigh.
Lonely hearts search for a flicker of flame,
Guided by memories, recalling a name.

Each word left unspoken, a soul's heavy weight,
Longing for solace, in doubt they await.
In corners of silence, their secrets reside,
Hurdles of anguish, where hope seems to hide.

Yet even in darkness, a flicker can thrive,
In the heart of the weary, dreams come alive.
Threads of redemption stitching the seams,
Bringing to light the forgotten old dreams.

For every prayer whispered without a reply,
There's a promise of morning, a forgiving sky.
When burdens feel heavy, and faith fades away,
The light will return, returning the day.

So gather these prayers, igniting the spark,
From ashes arise, through the long, velvet dark.
In the silence, remember, hope takes its flight,
For prayers forgotten shall find their own light.

Between the Altar and the Abyss

In shadows deep, our spirits plea,
The altar gleams, an oath we see.
With trembling hearts, we seek the light,
Yet glimpse the void of endless night.

Amidst the prayers, the silence falls,
Where angels tread, and darkness calls.
We dance on edges, faith and fear,
Between the sacred and the drear.

In whispered vows, our hopes ascend,
But doubts entwine, a bitter friend.
We stretch our hands to heaven high,
Yet feel the pull of shadows nigh.

Oh, guardian spirits, heed our cry,
As we navigate the watchful sky.
In sacred spaces, flaws are bare,
Yet love entwines in fervent prayer.

The light may fade, the whisper dim,
But hearts ignited, unable to swim.
Between the altar and the deep,
We seek the promise, yet we weep.

The Weeping Eye of Eternity

Beneath the stars, a tear flows free,
The weeping eye of eternity.
Lost in time, the moments cry,
Echoes of love that linger nigh.

In silence wrapped, our voices fade,
The weight of sorrows, debts unpaid.
From ashes rise, the spirit's flame,
Yet penance calls, and none to blame.

The cosmos swirls, a grand design,
Where hopes and dreams in shadows shine.
We cast our wishes on the air,
Yet find our hearts in disrepair.

Each moment lost, the price to pay,
Yet faith persists to guide our way.
In tears of starlight, paths unwind,
For in the dark, new love we find.

Oh, weeping eye, reflect our grace,
In every sorrow, there's a place.
Embrace the night, behold the dawn,
In every heart, the light is drawn.

Constellations of Regret and Yearning

In skies adorned with dreams long past,
Constellations form, a shadow cast.
Each star a wish we dared to keep,
Yet lost in promises, so deep.

With every turn, the heartache glows,
In diamond dust, our longing shows.
Through veils of doubt, our spirits strain,
As echoes whisper love and pain.

From distant worlds, our voices meet,
In cosmic dance, we find our feet.
But fleeting moments slip away,
Like stardust lost at break of day.

We search for signs in night's embrace,
In every heart, a sacred space.
Yet constellations fade in time,
As dreams dissolve in silent rhyme.

Yet hope persists, a guiding star,
In every wound, we heal from far.
Through regret's lens, we learn to see,
Yearning's voice, divine decree.

The Disharmony of Sacred Trust

In hallowed halls, we raise our plea,
Yet find within a disarrayed sea.
Promises scattered, like leaves in fall,
The fractures echo through the call.

In sacred bonds, our hearts entwined,
Yet shadows lurk, in fear confined.
We sigh for peace, in turmoil's grip,
With every word, our spirits slip.

In quest for truth, we wander lost,
Each burden carried, pain the cost.
Yet still we seek a glimmer bright,
In unity, to find our light.

Oh, sacred trust, where have you flown?
Amidst the chaos, we have grown.
Through storms we forge a bond anew,
Resilience found in love's pure view.

In disharmony, a lesson learned,
As fire rages, hearts are turned.
We rise from ashes, hope restored,
In every wound, our souls adored.

The Sorrow of a Faith Betrayed

In shadows deep, the heart does break,
A whispered prayer, for trust's own sake.
The sacred bond, now torn asunder,
Echoes of love, lost in life's thunder.

Once walked with grace, on holy ground,
Now silence fills, where hope was found.
Each tear that falls, a testament,
To faith transformed, no longer sent.

Oh, how the light, now fades away,
In doubt's embrace, it cannot stay.
Yet still I search, for signs of grace,
To mend the heart, in this dark place.

Forgive me, Lord, my faltering ways,
In despairing nights, I long for days.
When trust was whole, and love was pure,
But shadows loom, and hope's unsure.

So I stand here, with hands outstretched,
A broken soul, by sorrow fetched.
In faith's pursuit, I seek the light,
To guide me back, to what is right.

Celestial Echoes of the Unfaithful

In twilight's glow, the stars remain,
Once bright with hope, now stained with pain.
A heart that strays, from heaven's call,
Awaits the dawn, to break the fall.

Whispers of doubt, a haunting sigh,
In silent nights, beneath the sky.
The sacred truth, now hard to find,
As shadows wrap, around the mind.

Oh, fickle heart, why do you roam?
In search of love, you wander far from home.
Yet through the dark, a glimmer glows,
A path of light, where mercy flows.

The heavens weep, with gentle tears,
For every soul, that drifts in fears.
To seek the grace, that once was ours,
And find redemption, among the stars.

In every sigh, a prayer is made,
For weary hearts, that faith betrayed.
May echoes ring, in whispered pleas,
To mend the soul, and set it free.

A Pilgrim's Lament Beyond the Horizon

On distant shores, where hope is found,
A pilgrim walks, on sacred ground.
With every step, a prayer is sown,
In weary heart, seeds of hope grown.

The road is long, with trials steep,
But in the night, my soul will weep.
For every gain, a pain is shared,
In faith I tread, knowing I've bared.

In every dawn, a chance to rise,
To seek the truth, beyond the lies.
Though shadows loom, I press ahead,
With weary bones, on hope I'll tread.

My heart a compass, yearning still,
To find the peace, against my will.
Across the tides, my spirit yearns,
In every loss, for love that burns.

So guide me, Lord, through trials faced,
In every moment, my soul embraced.
For as I wander, I will believe,
Each step leads home, where hearts retrieve.

Chants of the Forgotten Covenant

Beneath the arches, voices rise,
In harmony, they seek the skies.
A covenant, once bright and clear,
Now whispers lost, to distant ear.

The promises made, in times of light,
Now fade to whispers, lost in night.
Yet still we sing, in hope we wait,
For love's return, to right the fate.

Forgotten vows, like autumn leaves,
Drift from the trees, while memory grieves.
In every note, a longing plea,
To reunite, our hearts set free.

So gather close, my weary kin,
In unity, we'll seek within.
For in our song, a spark remains,
To light the path, through all our pains.

Together we'll rise, with voices loud,
To rekindle faith, and make us proud.
With every chant, may love restore,
The forgotten bond, forevermore.

Dawning Hope

In the quiet morn, a whisper calls,
Softly breaking through night's deep thralls.
Hope awakens in the golden hue,
Guiding hearts to begin anew.

With every step, the shadows fade,
Faith ignites, no longer afraid.
In the warmth of light, we find our way,
Trusting the promise of a new day.

The sun ascends, a radiant sign,
In its glow, all souls intertwine.
Grace flows down like gentle rain,
Healing wounds, erasing pain.

Together we rise, hand in hand,
Walking forward on this holy land.
With each breath, we sing our song,
In the chorus of love, we all belong.

So let us cherish this dawning light,
Embracing joy that conquers night.
For in our hearts, the flame shall stay,
Illuminating the path each day.

Fading Light

As dusk approaches, shadows creep,
In the silence, the weary weep.
Memories linger, fading fast,
Echoes of a love that could not last.

The stars above begin to fade,
Whispers of hope seem less portrayed.
In a world where sorrows blend,
We seek the strength to comprehend.

Yet in the twilight, there's a spark,
A fragile flame in the dark.
Though light may dim, it does not die,
For in our hearts, we still believe nigh.

We gather fragments of the past,
Holding tightly till the last.
In fading light, we draw our dreams,
Finding solace in the moon's gentle beams.

So let us cherish the moments shared,
Even as the light is bared.
For in the darkness, we learn to see,
The beauty woven in our shared decree.

Through the Eyes of Broken Angels

Through shattered wings, the angels cry,
In their gaze, the world passes by.
With tender hearts, they wear their scars,
Carrying burdens beneath the stars.

Lost in the shadows, yet they soar,
Bearing wisdom from a distant shore.
In every tear, a story unfolds,
Of battles fought and dreams on hold.

Their voices sing of hope and grace,
In the quiet night, they find their place.
With every whisper, they mend the soul,
Binding wounds that make us whole.

They see the beauty in the pain,
Finding joy amidst the rain.
Through brokenness, they teach us to rise,
To find the light beneath our skies.

So may we learn from their embrace,
To seek the light in every trace.
For through the eyes of broken lore,
We find the strength to love once more.

The Weight of Unfulfilled Dreams

In the silence, dreams reside,
Heavy on the heart, they bide.
Visions once vibrant, now held tight,
Haunting us in the still of night.

With every breath, we taste the ache,
Each unfulfilled promise, a deep stake.
We search for meaning, yearn to see,
The purpose hidden in our decree.

Though paths diverge, and time moves on,
The weight of dreams is never gone.
In moments lost, we find the thread,
Rekindling hope for the days ahead.

So let the heart beat on in grace,
Embracing the journey, face to face.
For even dreams that slip away,
Help shape the light of our today.

With courage born from every pain,
We rise to dance in the fading rain.
For dreams may shift, but love endures,
In the depths of heart, it reassures.

Parched Soil of Untold Regrets

In barren fields, where silence reigns,
The weight of choices brings deep pains.
Each sigh echoes from the ground,
In parched soil, lost dreams abound.

We wander aimless, hearts laid bare,
Searching for water in the air.
Yet in the cracks, we find the signs,
Of life that lingers, hope entwines.

Beneath the surface, seeds still yearn,
For the rain to fall, the tides to turn.
Through every trial, wisdom grows,
In the desert of what we chose.

So let us plant with gentle hands,
The love that nurtures, life expands.
For even regret can bloom anew,
In the fertile ground of what we pursue.

With every tear that moistens soil,
We rise from depths, our spirits loyal.
Embracing growth, we find our grace,
In the journey's path, we find our place.

Torn Pages from the Book of Promises

In the whispers of the dawn's soft glow,
Pages flutter, secrets we can't know.
Each promise woven with threads of light,
In shadows cast, we seek the bright.

Beneath the weight of silent grief,
Faith stands tall, a steadfast relief.
With every tear, a story we mend,
In the book of hope, love shall transcend.

Echoes linger in the breath of time,
Each word a prayer, a sacred rhyme.
Torn but not broken, our spirits rise,
Guided by dreams that touch the skies.

For in the silence, God's voice resounds,
In hearts laid bare, true grace abounds.
Though pages torn may seem so flawed,
They speak of journeys walked with God.

So take these fragments, let them be,
A testament of our faith set free.
In the tapestry of life, we find,
That every page is intertwined.

When the Light of Faith Flickers

In the twilight where shadows creep,
A gentle whisper breaks the sleep.
When faith feels faint, and hope is lost,
We gather strength, no matter the cost.

Each candle burns, a guiding flame,
In the silence, we speak His name.
Though darkness looms and doubts invade,
In every heart, His love is laid.

Trust in the path that seems unclear,
For every struggle, He draws us near.
The flicker shines against the night,
A beacon bold, His endless light.

With every prayer, a promise made,
In the tapestry of faith displayed.
We rise as one, through trials and fears,
The light of love shines through our tears.

So hold on tight when shadows play,
For dawn will break, bring forth the day.
In the flickering, we find our song,
A melody of where we belong.

Hallowed Ground of Unkept Dreams

In fields of whispering winds and sighs,
Lay dreams unkept beneath vast skies.
With every heartbeat, a wish takes flight,
In the hallowed ground, we chase the light.

These visions weave through hopes untold,
The warmth of faith, a heart consoled.
Though burdens weigh like stones in a stream,
We walk with grace, embracing the dream.

In quiet moments, where prayers unfold,
Stories of courage in silence told.
Each tale a thread in life's grand design,
In the tapestry of souls divine.

Through valleys deep and mountains high,
We seek the truth, on wings we fly.
The path may twist, the road may bend,
Yet in His arms, we find our end.

So let us gather, hearts entwined,
In sacred spaces, love defined.
In unkept dreams, we find our creed,
In hallowed ground, our souls are freed.

The Burden of Forgotten Prayer

In the silence of the night, we weep,
For prayers forgotten, promises steep.
Each sigh a whisper, lost in the air,
The burden bears a weight we share.

Once fervent pleas now softly fade,
In shadows cast where hopes were laid.
Yet in the depths, His love remains,
A gentle touch through all our pains.

With every tear, a lesson learned,
In the quiet places, hearts have burned.
Though we may falter, our spirits heal,
In the essence of love, we rediscover zeal.

Gather the fragments, lift them high,
For in our weakness, He draws nigh.
The burden lightens with gratitude's grace,
In the power of prayer, we find our place.

So let go of doubts that cloud your sight,
For forgotten prayers still soar in flight.
In the sacred hush, we find our way,
Guided by love, come what may.

Chains of Faith Unraveled

In shadows deep, our spirits yearn,
For light that guides, for love to turn.
Each chain of doubt begins to break,
In whispered prayers, our hearts awake.

The covenant forged in trials fierce,
Brings forth the joy that fear cannot pierce.
With every tear, a promise sown,
In faith's embrace, we are not alone.

Mountains may rise, the storms may rage,
Yet in His arms, we turn the page.
With hands uplifted, we seek His grace,
In chains unbound, we find our place.

The journey long, the path unclear,
But through the darkness, He draws near.
In every struggle, His love displayed,
In chains of faith, our fears betrayed.

Our souls will sing, a boundless choir,
With hope ignited, our hearts on fire.
For chains once held now fall away,
In faith refined, we walk His way.

Lavished Grace

In morning light, His mercy flows,
Like rivers wide where no one knows.
Each drop a promise, soft and sweet,
In every heartbeat, He makes us complete.

The weary find their rest, their peace,
In simple grace, our doubts release.
For every sinner, a heart's embrace,
Through layers of love, we find our place.

In silent moments, He gently speaks,
To broken souls, to humble peaks.
With hands that heal and eyes of fire,
His grace surrounds, lifting us higher.

We dance through trials, we sing through pain,
In every storm, His love remains.
With lavish grace, He fills our days,
In gratitude, our souls we raise.

Though shadows linger, dim the light,
His presence guides through every night.
With every breath, we praise His name,
For lavished grace, our hearts aflame.

Withered Hope

In barren fields where dreams once grew,
The specter of despair, we pursue.
Each petal fallen, a whispered prayer,
With withered hope, we search for care.

Days stretch long under the weight of loss,
Each memory bitter, each pain a cross.
Yet in the dusk, a glimmer shines,
A fragile spark where hope aligns.

Through shattered visions, our spirits rise,
In brokenness, a chance to realize.
What seemed a void, now softly cradles,
A seed of faith that time unveils.

When hearts are weary and voices fade,
His promise lingers, never betrayed.
For in the silence, He hears our sighs,
With withered hope, our spirit flies.

Renewed in purpose, we learn to wait,
For dawn will break, it shan't be late.
With withered hope, new life will spring,
In every shadow, His praises sing.

Fraying Threads of Divine Trust

In gentle weavings of fate untold,
The threads of trust, both frail and bold.
Each strand a story, each knot a plea,
In fraying threads, we come to see.

A tapestry formed through trials faced,
With colors bright and shadows laced.
Through heartache's weave, His grace unfurls,
In frayed connections, our spirit swirls.

When questions linger, and doubts arise,
In every tear, a truth belies.
For even broken, He holds us fast,
In fraying threads, His love will last.

We gather strength from what is worn,
In every heartache, a promise born.
Through every struggle, we learn to trust,
In fraying threads, His love is just.

Our faith may waver, our spirits bend,
Yet in His arms, we find our friend.
With frayed but woven hearts, we stand,
In divine trust, held by His hand.

The Silent Penitence of Betrayed Hearts

In quiet chambers where shadows creep,
The silent cries of hearts that weep.
With sorrow wrapped in heavy sighs,
In betrayal's grasp, a soul's demise.

Yet forgiveness waits on mercy's shore,
A gentle tide that calls for more.
With open hands, we seek release,
In silent penitence, we find our peace.

Each whispered pain, a burdensome weight,
In currents of shame, we contemplate.
But love can mend what pride has torn,
From brokenness, a heart reborn.

When trust is shattered and bonds are thin,
In every fracture, grace pours in.
For even lost, we shall depart,
With silent penitence, a healing heart.

So let us gather, those who have strayed,
In unity rise, our fears outweighed.
For in the silence, redemption starts,
The silent penitence of betrayed hearts.

Heavenly Whispers

In the quiet dusk, angels sing,
Softly calling, their voices bring.
Heaven's breath upon our souls,
Guiding us toward sacred goals.

Stars alight in the night so clear,
Each twinkle holds a promise near.
In every prayer, a gentle spark,
Illuminating pathways dark.

With love divine, we walk this path,
Knowing grace will shield our wrath.
In trials strong, our spirits rise,
Trusting the truth that never lies.

Heavenly whispers, soft and sweet,
In their embrace, our hearts retreat.
Lost in the beauty, the peace we find,
Forever held by hands so kind.

Earthly Silence

In stillness lies the heart's true fight,
The whispers of the day take flight.
Beneath the weight of weary sighs,
A sacred space where courage lies.

Under the moon's gentle glow,
Where secrets dance and rivers flow.
Silence reigns in sacred halls,
A haven where the spirit calls.

Each breath we take, a prayer unsaid,
In the quiet, faith is fed.
We seek the truth in unvoiced lore,
Finding strength in the still, we soar.

In earthly grasp, we feel the sway,
Nature speaks, and we obey.
A bond with the earth, profound and grand,
In silence, we together stand.

The Fragrance of Faded Oaths

In shadows deep, our promise wane,
Like petals dropped from blooms of rain.
Echoes linger of vows once bright,
Lost in the folds of the endless night.

Through whispered winds, our hearts endure,
The fragrance sweet, a pain so pure.
In remembrance, we find our grace,
A journey carved in time and space.

What once was bold, now soft and frail,
Yet still, through storms, our spirits sail.
In the remnants of what we have sworn,
Faith's perfume, anew reborn.

Let not the past our hearts confine,
For love can bloom in every line.
The fragrance of oaths, both young and old,
A story woven in threads of gold.

Lamentations of the Waiting Heart

In quiet nights, the heart does grieve,
Awaiting signs that it believes.
With heavy tears, we look above,
Yearning for tales of grace and love.

Every moment, a prayerful sigh,
In shadows deep, we ask the sky.
The waiting heart, it longs for light,
Holding hope through darkest night.

Oft times we stumble, lost in the fray,
Yet faith endures, it paves the way.
Through trials grim, in storms we stand,
Embracing dreams with trembling hands.

In the hush, we catch a spark,
A whisper soft dispels the dark.
Lamentations melt to hope's warm fire,
In waiting's depth, we find desire.

Faith's Fragile Tapestry

Woven threads of joy and pain,
In faith's embrace, we break the chain.
Colors bright against the gray,
Each moment crafted in love's sway.

A tapestry stretched, both weak and strong,
In every stitch, we find our song.
In trials faced, we sew with care,
Building a quilt of heartfelt prayer.

The fabric holds our dreams and fears,
Stitched with laughter, shaded by tears.
In fragile beauty, hope is born,
Each thread a story, a sacred adorn.

When darkness falls and shadows creep,
Our faith remains, a promise deep.
Together we weave, in light's delight,
Faith's fragile tapestry shines bright.

Milton Keynes UK
Ingram Content Group UK Ltd.
UKHW020038271124
451585UK00012B/929

9 789916 791806